THE QUOTABLE DAD

THE
QUOTABLE
DAD

Compiled and with an introduction by
Tony Lyons and Nick Lyons

ISBN: 1-58574-277-4

2 4 6 8 10 9 7 5 3 1

Printed in the United States of America

The Library of Congress Cataloging-in-Publication
Data is available on file.

CONTENTS

INTRODUCTION

We've been connected as father and son for nearly forty years, so we've learned something about this eternally fascinating relationship; how it can be simultaneously rewarding and challenging.

In the beginning, there are a father's heightened expectations. A father's emotional response to a new offspring can be startling and unexpectedly intense, be it his first or fifth child. As child and father grow older, their world, and so their relationship, is constantly changing. All the complexities of life come into play; the dynamics of love, education, admiration, hope, pride, duty and delight fill the relationship with breadth and scope. The teenage years are rewarding and demanding for fathers, as they watch and help their children grow into adults.

Grown children bring still more rewards, as the family expands to include a wife and perhaps grandchildren, and sometimes, as happened to us, the opportunity to be in business together. Then there are those special moments when father and child can reflect and reminisce.

A tribute to the power of the paternal relationship is how much has been said and written on the subject. Writers of all stripes — psychologists, eminent statesmen, soldiers, artists and a host of others — have commented on the multidimensional nature of fatherhood. At times, their commentary has been wise, hilarious, practical and occasionally profound. We've enjoyed collecting some of the best of these words. We hope you enjoy this diverse collection of observations about fatherhood.

Tony & Nick Lyons
New York City
January 2001

TOP TEN QUOTES:

1) I felt something impossible for me to explain in words. Then when they took her away, it hit me. I got scared all over again and began to feel giddy. Then it came to me — I was a father.

NAT KING COLE

———◦◦◦———

2) I can run the country or control Alice [his daughter]. I can't do both.

THEODORE ROOSEVELT

3) Build me a son, O Lord, who will be strong enough to know when he is weak, and brave enough to face himself when he is afraid, one who will be proud and unbending in honest defeat, and humble and gentle in victory.

DOUGLAS MACARTHUR, "A FATHER'S PRAYER"

4) When Charles first saw our child Mary, he said all the proper things for a new father. He looked upon the poor little red thing and blurted, "She's more beautiful than the Brooklyn Bridge."

HELEN HAYES

5) The simplest toy, one which even the youngest child can operate, is called a grandparent.

SAM LEVENSON

6) My father gave me the greatest gift anyone could give another person. He believed in me.

JIM VALVANO

7) John Elway is a great football player. He used to be my son. Now I'm his father.

JACK ELWAY

8) When I was a kid, I used to imagine animals running under my bed. I told my dad, and he solved the problem quickly. He cut the legs off my bed.

LOU BROCK

⸻•⸻

9) You mustn't get aggravated when your old dad calls you his baby, because he always will think of you as just that — no matter how old or big you may get.

HARRY S TRUMAN, TO HIS DAUGHTER
MARGARET

⸻•⸻

10) You don't raise heroes, you raise sons. And if you treat them like sons, they'll turn out to be heroes if it's just in your own eyes.

WALTER M. SCHIRRA, SR.

1

On Becoming
a Father

We wanted you so badly. We loved you before we saw you.

> PETER CAREY, "A LETTER TO OUR SON,"
> THE GRANTA BOOK OF THE FAMILY

Some dads liken the impending birth of a child to the beginning of a great journey.

> MARCUS JACOB GOLDMAN, THE JOY OF
> FATHERHOOD

For fathers-to-be, pregnancy also serves as a time of profound transition: nine months of mental, emotional, material, perhaps physical, and almost certainly financial preparation to become a father.

KEVIN OSBORN, THE COMPLETE IDIOT'S GUIDE TO FATHERHOOD

———•◦◦◦•———

Arrange for paternity leave.

ANNIE PIGEON, DAD'S LITTLE INSTRUCTION BOOK

Many of us are not ready to be fathers when a child comes.

JOHN L. HART, BECOMING A FATHER

⸎

If you ever become a father, I think the strangest and strongest sensation of your life will be hearing for the first time the thin cry of your child.

LAFCADIO HEARN

... when my son looks up at me and breaks into his wonderful toothless smile, my eyes fill up and I know that having him is the best thing I will ever do.

DAN GREENBERG

———•◦•◦•———

There are times when parenthood seems nothing but feeding the mouth that bites you.

PETER DE VRIES

I felt something impossible for me to explain in words. Then when they took her away, it hit me. I got scared all over again and began to feel giddy. Then it came to me — I was a father.

NAT KING COLE

———◆·◆·◆———

"Is this kid beautiful, or is this kid beautiful."

I always ask to hear the choices again, because they sound so similar.

PAUL REISER, <u>COUPLEHOOD</u>

Fatherhood was a mysterious state and didn't seem to become any less so with time and familiarity. At night, when I looked in on my sleeping daughters, I would feel a deep sense of improbability mingled with inadequacy.

GEOFFREY NORMAN, <u>TWO FOR THE SUMMIT</u>

No man can possibly know what life means, what the world means, what anything means, until he has a child and loves it.

LAFCADIO HEARN

When dealing with a two-year-old in the midst of a tantrum, fathers need to be particularly watchful about the tendency to need to feel victorious.

DR. KYLE PRUETT (QUOTED IN DADS)

———•◆•———

When Charles first saw our child Mary, he said all the proper things for a new father. He looked upon the poor little red thing and blurted, "She's more beautiful than the Brooklyn Bridge."

HELEN HAYES

The best way to evaluate — and fine-tune — your childproofing efforts is to get down on your hands and knees and do a test run. Anything you can reach, your child can reach.

KEVIN OSBORN, THE COMPLETE IDIOT'S GUIDE TO FATHERHOOD

You look in the mirror and see the blurry image of two dads — one is tired, withered, drained, and pale, while the other is vibrant, enthusiastic, proud, and eager to meet the next challenge.

MARCUS JACOB GOLDMAN, THE JOY OF FATHERHOOD

I used to think having a dog was adequate preparation for parenthood, but I'm told they're not exactly the same — pet ownership and child rearing.

PAUL REISER, COUPLEHOOD

<hr />

. . . when I looked at you first I saw not your mother and me, but your two grandfathers . . . and, as my father, whom I loved a great deal, had died the year before, I was moved to see that here, in you, he was alive.

PETER CAREY, "A LETTER TO OUR SON,"
THE GRANTA BOOK OF THE FAMILY

The most important thing a father can do for his children is to love their mother.

THEODORE HESBURGH

———•◦•———

I cannot think of any need in childhood as strong as the need for a father's protection.

SIGMUND FREUD

Ideally, they should give you a couple of "practice kids" before you have any for real. Sort of like bowling a few frames for free before you start keeping score. Let you warm up.

PAUL REISER, COUPLEHOOD

———◦•▪•◦———

A young man asks an older musician, "How do I get to Carnegie Hall?" To which the older man answers, "Practice, my son, practice." You can say the same for fatherhood.

JEAN MARZOLLO, FATHERS AND BABIES

Fathers, provoke not your children to anger, lest they be discouraged.

THE HOLY BIBLE, COLOSSIANS 3:20

———

I grew up thinking my parents knew everything. I'm sure they didn't, but at least they were smart enough to fake it. I don't even know how to do that yet.

PAUL REISER, COUPLEHOOD

My children give me the gift of stepping out of the daily ordinariness into the father zone — a place where my innate curiosity, sense of adventure, and love of a weekend gets rediscovered.

JEFF STONE, "CONFESSIONS OF A WEEKEND DAD" (QUOTED IN DADS)

To show a child what once delighted you, to find the child's delight added to your own so that there is now a double delight seen in the glow of trust and affection, this is happiness.

J. B. PRIESTLEY

2

Fathers and

Daughters

The lucky man has a daughter as his first child.

SPANISH PROVERB (QUOTED IN TWO FOR THE
SUMMIT BY GEOFFREY NORMAN)

———— ❖ ————

When he saw his daughters happy he knew that he
had done well.

HONORÉ DE BALZAC, PÈRE GORIOT

A girl's father is the first man in her life, and probably the most influential.

DAVID JEREMIAH (QUOTED IN <u>FATHERS WHO DARE TO WIN</u> BY IAN GRANT)

———◆◆◆———

Daughters, I think, are always easier for fathers. I don't know why.

WILLIAM PLUMMER, <u>WISHING MY FATHER WELL</u>

She got the good looks from her father — he's a plastic surgeon.

GROUCHO MARX

———◦►◄◦———

A father is always making his baby into a little woman. And when she is a woman he turns her back again.

ENID BAGNOLD

I didn't have to do much, if anything, to rate a hug from one of my girls.

GEOFFREY NORMAN, <u>TWO FOR THE SUMMIT</u>

———

"Rose was like her father for all the world . . . she was always quoting her father — in fact, we used to call her 'Father says.'"

A CHILDHOOD FRIEND OF ROSE KENNEDY
(QUOTED IN <u>ROSE</u> BY GAIL CAMERON)

His sole pleasure was to gratify his daughters' whims . . . Goriot raised his daughters to the rank of angels, and so of necessity above himself.

HONORÉ DE BALZAC, PÈRE GORIOT

———

It isn't that I'm a weak father, it's just that she's a strong daughter.

HENRY FONDA

I can run the country or control Alice [his daughter].
I can't do both.

THEODORE ROOSEVELT

———◦•❖•◦———

... you want your daughters to adore you ... without reservation and without my doing anything to deserve it, for the sheer accidental reason that I was the only man in their young lives.

GEOFFREY NORMAN, TWO FOR THE SUMMIT

Many a man wishes he were strong enough to tear a telephone book in half — especially if he has a teenage daughter.

GUY LOMBARDO

Things not to worry about:

❏ Don't worry about popular opinion

❏ Don't worry about dolls

❏ Don't worry about the past

F. SCOTT FITZGERALD, TO HIS DAUGHTER SCOTTIE

True maturity is only reached when a man realizes he has become a father figure to his daughters' girlfriends — and he accepts it.

LARRY MCMURTRY

"All right, I'll give you fifty dollars to help pay your expenses for a couple of weeks, until you recover from this madness, but that's the last penny you'll get from me until you do something respectable."

THOMAS HEPBURN, TO HIS DAUGHTER
KATHARINE HEPBURN (QUOTED IN <u>FATHER KNEW BEST</u>)

It doesn't matter who my father was; it matters who I remember he was.

ANNE SEXTON

———❦———

"We are so young when we marry — what do we know of the world or of men? Our fathers ought to think for us."

DELPHINE TO HER FATHER IN PÈRE GORIOT BY HONORÉ DE BALZAC

My father taught me to be independent and cocky, and free thinking, but he could not stand it if I disagreed with him.

SARA MAITLAND

———•>•<•———

You mustn't get aggravated when your old dad calls you his baby, because he always will think of you as just that — no matter how old or big you may get.

HARRY S TRUMAN, TO HIS DAUGHTER
MARGARET

3

Fathers and

Sons

Like father, like son.

ANONYMOUS

———◆◆◆———

Build me a son, O Lord, who will be strong enough to know when he is weak, and brave enough to face himself when he is afraid, one who will be proud and unbending in honest defeat, and humble and gentle in victory.

DOUGLAS MACARTHUR, "A FATHER'S PRAYER"

A boy, by the age of 3 years, senses that his destiny is to be a man, so he watches his father particularly — his interests, manner, speech, pleasures, his attitude toward work . . .

BENJAMIN SPOCK AND MICHAEL B. ROTHENBERG, <u>DR. SPOCK'S BABY AND CHILD CARE</u>

———

'Tis a happy thing to be a father unto many sons.

WILLIAM SHAKESPEARE, <u>HENRY VI</u>

I like my boy . . . and his utter inability to conceive why I should not leave all my nonsense, business, and writing and come to tie up his toy horse . . .

RALPH WALDO EMERSON

———•◆•———

I enclose $1.00. Spend it liberally, generously, carefully, judiciously, sensibly. Get from it pleasure, wisdom, health, and experience.

EDWARD FITZGERALD, TO HIS SON F. SCOTT FITZGERALD (QUOTED IN FATHER KNEW BEST)

John Elway is a great football player. He used to be my son. Now I'm his father.

JACK ELWAY

———————

If my own son, who is now ten months, came to me and said, "You promised to pay for my tuition at Harvard; how about giving me $50,000 instead to start a little business," I might think that was a good idea.

WILLIAM BENNETT

A father follows the course of his son's life and notes many things of which he has not the privilege to speak.

WILLIAM CARLOS WILLIAMS, THE SELECTED LETTERS OF WILLIAM CARLOS WILLIAMS

———

. . . it's easy to wind back thirty or forty years to other times when Dad and I have been together in the woods beside a stream. It never really mattered where we were or whether we had caught many trout or found a lot of birds. Time and place were irrelevant as long as we shared them.

WILLIAM G. TAPPLY, SPORTSMAN'S LEGACY

My father would have enjoyed what you have so generously said of me — and my mother would have believed it.

LYNDON B. JOHNSON

———

There must always be a struggle between a father and son, while one aims at power and the other at independence.

SAMUEL JOHNSON

———

"I've taught you everything you know, but I haven't taught you everything I know."

IRA EARL ROBINSON

We think of our Fathers Fools, so wise we grow;

Our wiser Sons, no doubt, will think us so.

ALEXANDER POPE

———•◦•◦•———

I distrust any man who claims to have had a continu-
ous friendship with his father. How did he get from
fourteen to twenty-six?

VERLYN KLINKENBORG

Fathers send their sons to college either because they went to college or because they didn't.

L. L. HENDERSON

———•••———

The son hopes the father will talk to him. What he really hopes is that the suit of armor that is his father will teeter once or twice, creak, and fall over . . .

CHARLES GAINES

———•••———

You can't compare me to my father. Our similarities are different.

DALE BERRA, SON OF YOGI BERRA

I am delighted to have you play football. I believe in rough, manly sports. But I do not believe in them if they degenerate into the sole end of anyone's existence.

THEODORE ROOSEVELT, TO HIS SON
THEODORE ROOSEVELT, JR.

———◦•※•◦———

If the past cannot teach the present, and the father cannot teach the son, then history need not have bothered to go on, and the world has wasted a great deal of time.

RUSSELL HOBAN

Never fret for an only son. The idea of failure will never occur to him.

GEORGE BERNARD SHAW

———•◦•◦•———

[It was like] dealing with Dad — all give and no take.

JOHN F. KENNEDY, AFTER MEETING WITH KHRUSHCHEV

———•◦•◦•———

You don't raise heroes, you raise sons. And if you treat them like sons, they'll turn out to be heroes if it's just in your own eyes.

WALTER M. SCHIRRA, SR.

4
Father Knows
Best

———

My father didn't tell me how to live; he lived, and let me watch him do it.

CLARENCE KELLAND

My father instilled in me the attitude of prevailing. If there's a challenge, go for it. If there's a wall to break down, break it down.

DONNY OSMOND

The important thing, I learned from my father, was to find your own bone and sink your teeth in it.

WILLIAM PLUMMER, <u>WISHING MY FATHER WELL</u>

———❖———

My father told me there's no difference between a black snake and a white snake. They both bite.

THURGOOD MARSHALL

Do what you love, and love what you do.

MAURICE REDMOND HOLLOWAY

———•❖•———

Manual labor to my father was not only good and decent for its own sake but, as he was given to saying, it straightened out one's thoughts.

MARY ELLEN CHASE

My father used to say, "Let them see you and not the suit. That should be secondary."

CARY GRANT

———

My father had always said there are four things a child needs: plenty of love, nourishing food, regular sleep, and lots of soap and water. After that, what he needs most is some intelligent neglect.

IVY BAKER PRIEST

My father, who was in politics, told me to remain a bit mysterious. It makes people wonder about you, draws them to you as we are all drawn to a mystery.

JOE MILLS (QUOTED IN FROM FATHER TO SON, ALLEN APPEL)

———

My father was very sure about certain matters pertaining to the universe. To him, all good things — trout as well as eternal salvation — come by grace and grace comes by art, and art does not come easy.

NORMAN MACLEAN, A RIVER RUNS THROUGH IT

Moss Hart . . . once announced that in dealing with his children he kept one thing in mind: "We're bigger than they are, and it's our house."

JEAN KERR, PLEASE DON'T EAT THE DAISIES

From my mother I learned to make pie crusts and to iron shirts. From my father I learned to catnap and to tell time without a watch.

VERLYN KLINKENBORG

Parents should sit tall in the saddle and look upon their troops with a noble and benevolent and extremely nearsighted gaze.

GARRISON KEILLOR

⸻

A birthday is a good time to begin anew: throwing away the old habits, as you would old clothes, and never putting them on again.

BRONSON ALCOTT, TO HIS DAUGHTER ANNA

You're not a man until your father says you're a man.

BURT REYNOLDS

———

Father taught us that opportunity and responsibility go hand in hand. I think we all act on that principle; on the basic human impulse that makes a man want to make the best of what's in him and what's been given him.

LAURENCE ROCKEFELLER

Let us teach them not only to do virtuously, but to excel. To excel they must be taught to be steady, active, and industrious.

JOHN ADAMS, TO HIS WIFE ABIGAIL

———

My father gave me the greatest gift anyone could give another person. He believed in me.

JIM VALVANO

My father gave me these hints on speech-making: "Be sincere ... be brief ... be seated."

JAMES ROOSEVELT

———•◦•———

Above all, I would teach him to tell the truth ... Truth-telling, I have found, is the key to responsible citizenship. The thousands of criminals I have seen in forty years of law enforcement have had one thing in common: Every single one was a liar.

J. EDGAR HOOVER, "WHAT I WOULD TELL A SON"

As a Scot and a Presbyterian, my father believed that man by nature was a mess and had fallen from an original state of grace. Somehow, I early developed the notion that he had done this by falling from a tree.

NORMAN MACLEAN, <u>A RIVER RUNS THROUGH IT</u>

———◆———

Mind you, don't go looking for fights, but if you find yourself in one, make damn sure you win.

CLYDE MORRISON, TO HIS SON JOHN WAYNE (QUOTED IN <u>FATHER KNEW BEST</u>)

When I was a kid, I used to imagine animals running under my bed. I told my dad, and he solved the problem quickly. He cut the legs off my bed.

LOU BROCK

———

I'm your father, that's why.

BRUCE LANSKY AND K. L. JONES, DADS SAY THE DUMBEST THINGS

I hope when you grow up, you will dedicate your life to trying to work out plans to make people happy instead of making them miserable, as war does today.

JOSEPH P. KENNEDY, TO HIS SON EDWARD, AGE 8

———•••———

This above all: to thine own self be true, and it must follow, as the night the day, thou canst not then be false of any man.

POLONIUS, TO HIS SON LAERTES, IN HAMLET BY WILLIAM SHAKESPEARE

My dad has always taught me these words: care and share.

TIGER WOODS

———

Dad often said, "A man that doesn't pick up a penny that's laying on the ground won't ever amount to much."

RIC ANDERSON (QUOTED IN FROM FATHER TO SON, ALLEN APPEL)

———

I have never smoked. I have my father to thank for that.

JIMMY CARTER, EVERYTHING TO GAIN

As you journey through [life], you will encounter all sorts of these nasty little upsets, and you will either learn to adjust yourself to them or gradually go nuts.

GROUCHO MARX, TO HIS SON ARTHUR

So subtle were his teachings, though, that I never knew they were his until I became a parent myself and saw my father in me as I began to shape my own children's lives.

KENNETH BARRETT

The best advice ever given me was from my father. When I was a little girl, he told me, "Don't spend anything unless you have to."

DINAH SHORE

——•••——

I expect I must, in part, have developed my notion of character from watching my father struggle against the mesquite.

LARRY MCMURTRY, <u>WALTER BENJAMIN AT THE DAIRY QUEEN</u>

. . . and while I want you to keep looking well, I think that if you spent a little more time picking up your clothes instead of leaving them on the floor, it wouldn't be necessary to have them pressed so often.

JOSEPH P. KENNEDY, TO HIS SON JACK, AGE 14

Neither a borrower nor a lender be;

For loan oft loses both itself and friend,

And borrowing dulls the edge of husbandry.

POLONIUS, TO HIS SON LAERTES, IN HAMLET
BY WILLIAM SHAKESPEARE

My father taught me that the only way you can make good at anything is to practice, and then practice some more.

PETE ROSE

⸺◦⟡◦⸺

How true Daddy's words were when he said: "All children must look after their own upbringing."

ANNE FRANK

⸺◦⟡◦⸺

What a father says to his children is not heard by the world; but it will be heard by posterity.

JEAN PAUL RICHTER

5

A Hard

Profession

We are given children to test us and make us more spiritual.

GEORGE F. WILL

———•••———

How children survive being brought up amazes me.

MALCOLM S. FORBES

Like any father, I have moments when I wonder whether I belong to the children or they belong to me.

BOB HOPE

———◦•✦•◦———

Remember: fatherhood is a work in progress.

ANNIE PIGEON, DAD'S LITTLE INSTRUCTION BOOK

Insanity is hereditary; you can get it from your children.

SAM LEVENSON

⸺ ⬥ ⸺

My father the banker would shudder to see

In the back of his bank a painter to be.

PAUL CÉZANNE

I was the same kind of father as I was a harpist — I played by ear.

HARPO MARX

Unfortunately, children don't come already trained, and whether we like it or not, they will sometimes develop habits and attitudes which we need to train them out of!

IAN GRANT, FATHERS WHO DARE TO WIN

Fatherhood, for me, has been less a job than an unstable and surprising combination of adventure, blindman's bluff, guerrilla warfare, and crossword puzzle.

FREDERIC F. VAN DE WATER

Reasoning with a child is fine, if you can reach the child's reason without destroying your own.

JOHN MASON BROWN (QUOTED IN THE BEST OF FATHER QUOTATIONS, ED. HELEN EXLEY)

I can always count on getting one thing for Father's Day — all the bills from Mother's Day.

MILTON BERLE

———— ·—◦—· ————

Children of the new millennium when change is likely to continue and stress will be inevitable, are going to need, more than ever, the mentoring of an available father.

IAN GRANT, FATHERS WHO DARE TO WIN

By profession I am a soldier and take great pride in that fact, but I am also prouder, infinitely prouder, to be a father. A soldier destroys in order to build; the father only builds, never destroys.

DOUGLAS MACARTHUR, REMINISCENCES

———•••———

Fatherhood has been known to transform even the toughest and most resilient into a quivering mass.

MARCUS JACOB GOLDMAN, THE JOY OF FATHERHOOD

To be happy, fathers must always be giving; it is ceaselessly giving that makes you really a father.

GORIOT, IN <u>PÈRE GORIOT</u> BY HONORÉ DE BALZAC

———•+•+•———

Life doesn't come with an instruction book — that's why we have fathers.

H. JACKSON BROWNE'S DAD (AS QUOTED IN <u>A FATHER'S BOOK OF WISDOM</u>)

It takes time to be a good father. It takes effort —
trying, failing, and trying again.

TIM HANSEL (AS QUOTED IN DAD'S
APPRECIATION BOOK OF WIT AND WISDOM)

This is the hardest truth for a father to learn: that his
children are continuously growing up and moving
away from him (until, of course, they move back in).

BILL COSBY, FATHERHOOD

A king, realizing his incompetence, can either delegate or abdicate his duties. A father can do neither.

MARLENE DIETRICH (QUOTED IN <u>DADS</u>)

In America there are two classes of travel — first class and with children.

ROBERT BENCHLEY

The lone father is not a strong father. Fathering is a difficult and perilous journey and is done well with the help of other men.

JOHN L. HART, BECOMING A FATHER

———•••———

Raising children is part joy and part guerrilla warfare.

ED ASNER

If the new American father feels bewildered and even defeated, let him take comfort from the fact that whatever he does in any fathering situation has a fifty percent chance of being right.

BILL COSBY

No, you can't charge them rent when they're still in grade school.

ANNIE PIGEON, DAD'S LITTLE INSTRUCTION BOOK

A father is a man who is always learning to love. He knows that his love must grow and change because his children change.

TIM HANSEL (AS QUOTED IN DAD'S APPRECIATION BOOK OF WIT AND WISDOM)

—◦•◦—

Mostly you just have to keep plugging and keep loving — and hoping that your child forgives you according to how you loved him, judged him, forgave him, and stood watching over him as he slept, year after year.

BEN STEIN, "MISTAKES OF THE FATHER"
QUOTED IN DADS

You know the only people who are always sure about the proper way to raise children? Those who've never had any.

BILL COSBY, <u>FATHERHOOD</u>

———•···•———

. . . if you see the challenge of fathering as the biggest victory of your life, it will be a goal worth stretching for.

IAN GRANT, <u>FATHERS WHO DARE TO WIN</u>

6

Appreciating

Dad

———

Directly after God in heaven comes papa.

W. A. MOZART

———————

A father is a banker provided by nature.

FRENCH PROVERB

His values embraced family, reveled in the social mingling of the kitchen, and above all, welcomed the loving disorder of children!!!

JOHN COLE

—•◦•◦•—

One father is more than a hundred schoolmasters.

GEORGE HERBERT

Fatherhood was full-time work for Dad. When I was about ten, I took up the clarinet. Instead of buying me a metronome and sending me off to a soundproof room to squeak my way through the scales, he sat with me and beat time against the arm of his chair with his pipe.

WILLIAM G. TAPPLY, <u>SPORTSMAN'S LEGACY</u>

I talk and talk and talk, and I haven't taught people in fifty years what my father taught by example in one week.

MARIO CUOMO

My father is my idol, so I always did everything like him. He used to work two jobs and still come home happy every night. He didn't do drugs or drink, and he wouldn't let anyone smoke in his house. Those are the rules I adopted, too.

EARVIN "MAGIC" JOHNSON

The search for a father is a search for authority outside of yourself; you feel wraithlike, incomplete without him, in whatever form he takes.

NICK LYONS

———•◦•———

When he first thought about him it was always the eyes . . . they saw much further and much quicker than the human eye sees and they were the great gift his father had. His father saw as a bighorn ram or as an eagle sees, literally.

ERNEST HEMINGWAY, "FATHERS AND SONS"

My father was a statesman. I'm a political woman. My father was a saint. I'm not.

INDIRA GANDHI

———◦•◦———

My father was not a failure. After all, he was the father of a president of the United States.

HARRY S TRUMAN

. . . it took me years to recognize my father's depths, how I am sounding them still. . . . All I ever saw, growing up, was his difference from me.

WILLIAM PLUMMER, <u>WISHING MY FATHER WELL</u>

———◦⋅▪⋅◦———

When I was fourteen, my father was so ignorant I could hardly stand to have the old man around. But when I got to be twenty-one, I was astonished at how much he had learned in seven years.

MARK TWAIN

7
The Later
Years

The simplest toy, one which even the youngest child can operate, is called a grandparent.

SAM LEVENSON

———•◦•◦•———

By the time a man realizes that maybe his father was right, he usually has a son who thinks he's wrong.

CHARLES WADSWORTH

———•◦•◦•———

The greatest legacy a man can leave in the world is not so much a great business, but a "living" investment in the future, through loving, stable, employable and healthy children.

IAN GRANT, FATHERS WHO DARE TO WIN

What you have inherited from your father, you must earn over again for yourselves, or it will not be yours.

JOHANN WOLFGANG VON GOETHE

———

I suppose you think that persons who are as old as your father and myself are always thinking about very grave things, but I know that we are meditating on the same old themes that we did when we were ten years old, only we go more gravely about it.

H. D. THOREAU, TO ELLEN EMERSON, R. W. EMERSON'S DAUGHTER

My father died at 102. Whenever I would ask what kept him going, He'd answer, "I never worry."

JERRY STILLER, MARRIED TO LAUGHTER

———————

Nothing I've ever done has given me more joys and rewards than being a father to my five.

BILL COSBY, FATHERHOOD

———————

Some day you will know that a father is much happier in his children's happiness than in his own. I cannot explain it to you: it is a feeling in your body that spreads gladness through you.

HONORÉ DE BALZAC, PÈRE GORIOT

What I learned is that if I don't know something, I just shrug my shoulders and admit it. Doctors don't know everything. Neither do teachers. Or dads.

FRANK MCCOURT (QUOTED IN <u>DADS</u>)

And though I know we are different, I am grateful for what I have of my father in me. It is my gift, my promise to myself and my children.

KENNETH BARRETT

By the time the youngest children have learned to keep the house tidy, the oldest grandchildren are on hand to take it to pieces.

CHRISTOPHER MORLEY

———

A man knows when he is growing old because he begins to look like his father.

GABRIEL GARCÍA MÁRQUEZ

Every generation revolts against its fathers and makes friends with its grandfathers.

LEWIS MUMFORD

———•◦•———

Grandparents range from infantile to mature, like everybody else.

JEAN MARZOLLO, FATHERS AND BABIES

One of life's greatest mysteries is how the boy who wasn't good enough to marry your daughter can be the father of the smartest grandchild in the world.

JEWISH PROVERB

He is tender and wary with his grandson, this messenger of life and his mortality.

MICHAEL IGNATIEFF, "AUGUST IN MY FATHER'S HOUSE," THE GRANTA BOOK OF THE FAMILY

———•◦•◦•———

You've got to do your own growing, no matter how tall your grandfather was.

IRISH PROVERB

Dad and I never run out of things to talk about, but I am content that he and I have said everything that needs saying already. It's never been hard.

WILLIAM G. TAPPLY, SPORTSMAN'S LEGACY

———

When you teach your son, you teach your son's son.

THE TALMUD

INDEX

My Memories of Dad

My Memories of Dad

My Memories of Dad

My Memories of Dad

My Memories of Dad

My Memories of Dad

My Memories of Dad

My Memories of Dad

My Memories of Dad

My Memories of Dad

_____

_____

_____

_____

_____

_____

_____

_____

_____

_____

_____

_____

_____

_____

_____

_____

_____

_____

My Memories of Dad

My Memories of Dad

My Memories of Dad

My Memories of Dad

My Memories of Dad

My Memories of Dad

My Memories of Dad

My Memories of Dad

My Memories of Dad

My Memories of Dad

My Memories of Dad

My Memories of Dad